# BASIC STRING REPAIRS

*Basic tools and equipment*

1. Peg-shaping block, soap, and sandpaper. 2. Wheelbrace, with two twist drills. 3. Archimedes or fretwork drill, and bits. 4. Small saw. 5. Bridge-fitting guide with abrasive sheets. 6. Penknife. 7. Knife-edge file. 8. Round, needle-point files. 9. Smooth file, eight or ten inches. 10. Scissors. 11. Tube of glue. 12. Pliers. 13. Violin cramp (belly or back to ribs).

# BASIC STRING REPAIRS

*A guide for string-class teachers*

ARTHUR BURGAN

LONDON
OXFORD UNIVERSITY PRESS
NEW YORK TORONTO
1974

*Oxford University Press, Ely House, London W.*1

GLASGOW NEW YORK TORONTO MELBOURNE WELLINGTON
CAPE TOWN IBADAN NAIROBI DAR ES SALAAM LUSAKA ADDIS ABABA
DELHI BOMBAY CALCUTTA MADRAS KARACHI LAHORE DACCA
KUALA LUMPUR SINGAPORE HONG KONG TOKYO

ISBN 0 19 318509 1

*Printed in Great Britain by
The Camelot Press Ltd, London and Southampton*

# CONTENTS

# LIST OF PLATES

# INTRODUCTION

The repairing of stringed instruments is, like many other crafts, a dying art, and repairers are few and far between. At the same time, the playing of stringed instruments has for a number of years been on the increase, with a consequent upsurge in the number of damaged instruments. This is a special problem for string-class teachers, since they are dealing simultaneously with a number of instruments. They now wait for weeks or months for their repairs to be attended to, and the cost to the local authorities is no mean figure.

I have been for many years a string-class teacher and for part of that time the repairer for Hull Education Authority, and it has become increasingly clear to me that this state of affairs can only be improved if the teachers themselves are prepared to carry out minor repairs and adjustments wherever possible.

Since the majority of teachers are probably unversed in the use of tools, a highly technical handbook would be of no use whatsoever. So I have endeavoured to set out as clearly as I can the steps to take when performing simple repairs and adjustments. I have also mentioned and illustrated two pieces of equipment which I have made, the peg shaper and the bridge fitting guide (provisional patent applied for), since the sophisticated tools used by the repairer would be beyond the scope of the amateur.

I trust that what I have written will be of some use to those who are willing to try their hand at rectifying the everyday mishaps which we have all met at some time or another.

A. B.

# CHAPTER 1

## PREVENTION IS BETTER THAN CURE

A great deal of frustration and annoyance on the part of the teacher, and possible expense to the parents or local authorities, not to mention practice missed by the pupil, could be saved by the proper care of instruments. It is no good saying to a child who brings an instrument with a peg or some other part broken, 'Your father shouldn't have tried to tune it.' If this happens to any of us as string-class teachers, then we are too late.

It is during the first few lessons that we must instil into the pupils the need for care in handling their instruments, and this theme must be maintained *ad infinitum*, because good habits in the handling of instruments, if inculcated from the very beginning, will help to eliminate some of the breakages which occur through lack of training. For example, in the first lesson, when the pupils have removed the violins from their cases to sit in the 'resting' position (i.e. with the violin under the right arm), they must be warned about the danger of damage to their instruments if they suddenly lean back and knock the tail-piece end against the chair. Also, if pupils are trained to keep their nails short there will be less chance of scratches on the belly of the instrument.

Perhaps I might say a few words on how I arrange the seating in my classes.

Assuming that one has, say, a class of eight violin pupils, they sit in two rows of four, leaving enough space between the chairs for the case to go on the floor with the 'narrow end to the front', on the right of the pupil. For the first lesson or so it is no use referring to the 'scroll' end of the case, as the pupils do not yet know which end this is. The reason for putting the case in this position is that the child can easily lift out the instrument in the correct way, with his left hand under the neck. He can then rest the instrument on his knees with the strings facing him, and is able to see it all very clearly. There must be enough space between the rows to enable the back row to stand facing a music stand. This may all seem very obvious, but I have seen it otherwise!

Cases should remain on the floor at all times, and you must emphasize the necessity for checking that they are *fastened* before being moved. It is easy to imagine what would happen to an instrument if a child suddenly started running to catch a bus, having been careless in fastening the case.

If pupils are allowed to leave cases on tables or desks, sooner or later the odds are that an instrument or bow will be damaged, as a result of general movement about the room.   Incidentally, cellists must be warned about taking the bow out of its pocket in a canvas or similar type of cover, *before* removing the cover from the instrument. Also, when taking out the end-pin, pupils should hold the cello with the left hand round the neck, with the back of the instrument towards the body, and the lower part resting on the pupil's thigh. This is partly to prevent damage to anyone who may be moving past, especially during an orchestral rehearsal! Another point is that during rehearsals, or whenever the cello is placed on its side on the floor for more than a few seconds, the end-pin must be pushed in, as people walking past do not always see it sticking out.

When pupils do their practice at home, they should always put the bow on a flat surface such as a table, sideboard, or piano if available, but never on a chair. I remember some years ago a boy who, during a practice session at home, put his cello on its back on a settee. Shortly afterwards, he sat on the settee, having forgotten that the cello was there! Incredible, but true, resulting in cracks over one foot long in both back and front. I hasten to add that he was not a pupil of mine!

There are times during the first few months of lessons when one can easily be tempted into thinking that pupils must be tired of our constant reiteration of the same theme —'take care', and so on. But beware, keep it up, and you will be rewarded by having fewer bridges to renew, broken bows to replace, and the like.

With regard to care of the bow, I suggest that teachers should tell their pupils never to remove it from the case unless told to do so. This is to guard against the over-zealous parent who, to 'help' his child, may take out the bow and screw it up with dire results: the bow may lose its spring, the stick may break, or the button may come right off the shank of the screw itself. (See p. 38.)

To avoid this, teachers should tell their pupils, not simply 'Tighten the bow'—which to a child means just that —but, more specifically, 'Turn the screw until the space between the hair and the stick at the narrowest point is just wide enough to get a pencil through (or, just the same width as the thickness of the stick).' A problem arises when telling pupils to do this if the stick has been left tightened up for too long and, as a result, has lost its spring and become straight. One can readily understand, therefore, how important it is for the pupils to tighten their bows only just enough, and to slacken them off immediately after playing. Should a bow lose its spring it can be rectified by re-springing. This I have dealt with in Chapter 5.

When putting the bow away pupils should see that the hair is downwards when the bow is in the bottom of the lid, and upwards when at the top. This is to prevent the hair becoming entangled with the adjusters when the lid is closed. A duster wrapped round the instrument helps, but is not sufficient by itself.

Whilst on the subject of adjusters, always keep the adjusting screw well clear of the belly. Scratches on the varnish and, in extreme cases, holes in the belly, are silent testimony to this glaring omission.

Occasionally the protective covering on the spring clip which holds the bow in position will wear off. The resultant damage to the instrument has to be seen to be believed: a large hollow scooped out of the belly on the E side of the tail-piece. A few moments spent putting on a strip of adhesive tape of the cloth type will prevent this happening.

Before tuning violins I always look at the bridge from two angles:

(1) Sideways, to make sure that it is not leaning forward and therefore ready to collapse at any time.

(2) From the front, to see that it is midway between the $f$ holes and that the strings are, therefore, equally spaced on the fingerboard.

A child, in his eagerness to reach home, can, without being aware of it, give the case a knock which will move the bridge as much as $\frac{1}{2}''$ sideways. Incidentally, instruments must never be placed on luggage racks in buses or trains since, apart from the obvious possibility of forgetting them, there is a risk of damage being caused if a heavy suitcase falls on the instrument.

A special word to all those who teach the cello. Because of its size, sometimes out of all proportion to the size of the pupil carrying it, this instrument is very prone to damage, especially in the lower bouts. If a child is carrying the cello by the handle on the cover, the lower bout of the instrument is very close to the ground. As he steps downwards off the pavement in order to cross a road, or goes down stairs, this part of the cello is, therefore, behind him and will either hit the edge of the pavement or bounce off every step. This is not calculated to do the instrument any good! All this can happen again when stepping upwards from the road to the pavement, and the greater the distance between the two, the greater the risk of damage.

Consider what a multitude of very solid objects protrude into a pupil's path—telegraph poles, lamp standards, Belisha beacons, traffic bollards, cycle racks, and vending machines. All these constitute serious hazards to a child who is carrying a cello which could sustain quite serious damage if knocked against any one of them.

Another vitally important point in connection with cellos is the end-pin. The end-pin must have a collar on it, near the point, to prevent the pin from dropping into the instrument. When this happens, and it does, the end-pin goes right through the ribs somewhere near where they are joined on to the neck, and the result is a jagged hole to be repaired which should not have to be done.

The question of storage of instruments in school, particularly cellos and double basses, can present enormous problems, so I would suggest three ways of storing these two instruments:

(1) Stand them in a corner, with the strings inwards. The end-pin must be kept sharp, to prevent the instrument from slipping.

(2) Stand them with their backs against shelves or a wall, with two pieces of wood projecting outwards at right angles, the space in between them being wide enough to take the neck of a cello or double bass. The instrument is held in position by a strap with a buckle which fastens round the front of the neck.

(3) Lay them down on their edges. In this case, and in fact whenever a cello or double bass has to be moved from this position, for example at a rehearsal, insist that the pupil *lifts* the instrument instead of simply sliding it along the floor, as the latter soon wears the edges of the belly,

which, of course, is made of much softer wood than the back, and they soon become splintered or broken.

When storing instruments at home, the pupils should be told to stand them in a corner or lay them on their side, and also to keep their instruments well out of reach of small children or pets.

N.B.—All instruments, whether stored in schools or at home, should be kept away from any source of direct heat, such as fires or radiators. Care must also be taken to ensure that instruments are not, at any time, subject either to direct sunlight or to extremes of cold.

One final word about rosin, and its application on the bow. I am sure we are all familiar with the cake of rosin which has a groove worn down the middle, followed in time by another groove at right angles to the first one, leaving four corners standing up which are eventually thrown away, wasting half of the block. This unnecessary waste could be avoided by the simple expedient of rotating the rosin whilst the bow is being rubbed on it. Also, I find it is a good plan to hold the bow in such a way that the first finger and thumb of the right hand just cover the ferrule to prevent it from hitting the rosin and chipping it round the edges. Incidentally, all pupils should be taught the habit of dusting their instruments and bow sticks each time they are used, in order to keep them free from rosin dust.

## GENERAL HINTS

Fasteners on violin and viola cases must be effective. If in doubt put a strap round the case, taking it underneath the handle.

When instruments are carried by pupils who cycle to school, a harness made of webbing, enabling the case to be carried on the back, is particularly useful. Perhaps these sketches may be helpful.

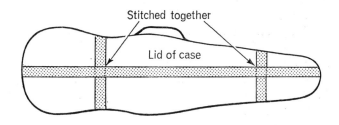

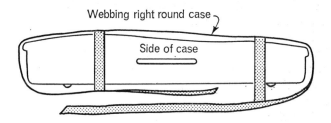

*Underneath the case, the two ends must be left long enough to go over the shoulder and fasten with a buckle, or something which cannot come apart*

Do not carry music, sandwiches, or anything but an instrument in its case.

Keep fingers, and in fact everything except rosin, off bow hair.

Before the hair becomes very dirty it can be cleaned with Polyclens or similar liquid, then washed with soap, thoroughly rinsed, and left to dry. Try to keep water away from the wedges in the frog and head of the bow and, when drying the hair, leave the bow lying down. This is to prevent the wedges from swelling owing to the absorption of water, and possibly splitting the frog or head of the bow.

When instruments are supplied with bows which have no rosin on them, one can rub them with powdered rosin, easily obtained by crushing a few bits of broken rosin, always readily available, with a knife.

Always have a name and address in the case. Cellists can tie a label on the handle of the cover. If the instrument is privately owned the address can be permanently fixed to the case, but for instruments which are on loan, a label in the compartment where rosin, mute, etc., are kept is perhaps better.

Music should not be rolled or folded and put into a violin or viola case. Apart from the fact that music thus treated will not lie flat on a music stand, there is the risk of damage to the instrument.

In the event of metal strings digging their way into a bridge, due, perhaps, to the absence of bridge protectors, or to the fact that the wood of which the bridge is made is softer than it should be, we eventually find that the strings are too near the fingerboard. This means that the strings vibrate on the fingerboard when stopped notes are played, and occasionally the strings will be too 'flat' to play on separately, in the sense that there is not sufficient curve on the top of the bridge. If the two middle strings are lower than they should be, that is, too near the finger-board, they can be raised by putting a small piece of *thin* leather on the bridge under the string.

If the bridge itself is too low, and the string spacings are correct, it can be raised by cutting thin pieces of card and putting them under the feet of the bridge. This is quite an adequate temporary measure, until such time as a new bridge can be fitted. The Art and Craft department in schools will normally be pleased to help in supplying card of varying thicknesses, and will probably oblige in permitting the use of a guillotine.

Should a metal string break at the ball end, do not throw it away, but tie a half knot on the end where it has snapped and bend up at right angles the $\frac{1}{4}''$ or so of the string which will be sticking out from the knot, thus:

When the string is tuned for playing, this will prevent the end of the string from slipping out. I have found that this can be done quite successfully even on a cello.

If you are experiencing frequent breakages of strings in the peg box (or above the fingerboard nut) it would be advisable in the case of three-quarter- and half- size instruments—especially violins—to prepare for this contingency by leaving the new string at its normal full length, instead of cutting it short in order to reduce the number of turns of string round the peg. This will give you more string to play with, should it be necessary to tie knots above the fingerboard nut. On instruments less than half-size you will almost certainly have to cut off a portion of a new string as they are always too long.

Should an excess of rosin accumulate on the belly of an instrument or bow stick it can be cleaned off quite successfully with Polyclens (but test this first on a portion of the ribs near the end-pin). Then wipe with a damp cloth and polish with violin polish.

# CHAPTER 2

## FITTING PEGS—VIOLIN AND VIOLA

We have all, at some time or other, seen and heard badly fitting pegs. These rather neglected pieces of wood have a vitally important task to perform—that of holding the strings firmly in position, while allowing easy turning when tuning the instrument.

First of all, let us look at the scroll, or peg-box. There are two holes for each peg, and it is not always realized that they taper slightly, the wider side being where the peg enters. This tapering can, normally, only be achieved by the use of a peg-hole reamer which, if used, should be handled with great care, otherwise the hole will become too large and necessitate 'bushing', which is a job for a repairer. The reamer and peg shaper used by violin makers and repairers are, as a rule, too expensive for the teacher to buy, as he or she will most probably be fitting pegs only on rare occasions. The device illustrated in Plate 1 is, therefore, intended for use by the teacher who does not possess more elaborate items of equipment, and it can be used very effectively in fitting pegs. (See Coda.)

Before starting to fit a peg, it is wise to reflect for a few moments about the shape of that portion of the peg on which you are going to work. It appears to be round, and in fact when newly made will be perfectly round. However, as most pegs are made of wood—rosewood, ebony, boxwood, or, in the case of cheaper pegs, softwood stained black to simulate ebony—they are naturally prone to shrinkage. Therefore by the time you come to fit them, they will, in all probability, be slightly elliptical in shape. Although it is

possible to obtain plastic pegs nowadays they are a very
poor substitute for the wooden pegs mentioned above,
and are not to be recommended. Neither, for that matter,
are the black-stained softwood type, as they have a nasty
habit of breaking off close to the peg-box.

Now you are ready to fit the peg.

(1) Place the peg in the slot, holding the peg between
the thumb and first finger of the left hand.

(2) Rotate the peg smoothly and at the same time rub
with the sandpaper block, taking care to ensure that the
sandpaper is used only while the peg is being turned, otherwise flat sides will result on the peg and it will not fit
the hole as it should.

(3) Check the fit of the peg frequently using a piece of
dry soap as a lubricant and you will see shiny surfaces on
the parts of the peg which are actually touching the holes.
(See Plate 2.) To gauge the correct length of the peg
(assuming that one is fitting an isolated peg), the distance
to the inner edge of the thumb piece from the outer cheek
of the peg-box should match the other pegs. If one is
fitting a complete set of pegs this distance should be
$\frac{7}{10}''$ (18 mm.).

(4) It now only remains for the surplus wood to be cut
off the end of the peg, using either a knife or a fine saw,
taking care to cut all round the peg a little at a time, or
else there will be a risk of splitting it. Now the end can be
smoothed with sandpaper, finishing off with what is known
as flourpaper. The end of the peg should be slightly convex,
and when inserted into its holes, this rounded end should
project just beyond the surface of the peg-box. The end can
also be given a final polish by moistening it and rubbing
with a soft cloth. (See Plate 3.)

(5) A hole must now be drilled for the string at a distance
of about $\frac{1}{8}''$ (3–4mm.) from the inside of the peg-box. A
$\frac{1}{16}''$ diameter (2 mm.) hole is quite satisfactory for a violin

or viola; a larger hole, big enough to take a C string, will, of course, be needed for the cello. The type of drill called a wheel-brace, or an Archimedes drill, is most suitable for this operation (the latter is perhaps cheaper to buy), but the peg must not be allowed to move, and consequently must be held very firmly either by the hands of an assistant, or by the jaws of a vice on which pieces of soft leather have been placed to prevent damage to the peg, or, failing both of these, in the groove of the peg-shaping block illustrated in Plate 4, the pressure from the drill preventing it from moving whilst the drilling is being done.

The greatest care must be exercised when drilling and the following points must be observed:

(*a*) Position the drill exactly in the centre of the peg, thus:

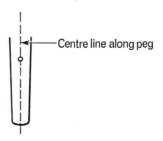

Centre line along peg

(*b*) Keep the wheelbrace upright, in such a way that the drill will come through in the centre of the peg on the opposite side.

(*c*) Do not press hard, or the peg is liable to splinter when the drill goes through.

(*d*) Using a rat-tail file, rub gently on the hole at right angles to the peg, to remove the sharp edges, thus:

This helps to prevent strings breaking at a point where it is not always possible to repair them by tying a knot.

A final rub with an oily rag is all that is required to complete the fitting of a peg.

Of the three types of wood mentioned at the beginning of this chapter, great care must be taken in the handling of ebony because, whilst it is hard, it is also very brittle, and splinters easily.

Incidentally, boxwood is a very hard, dense, and close-grained wood and is not to be confused with 'box wood', which is usually cheap quality softwood used, as the name implies, in the manufacture of boxes.

Perhaps a word here about putting on a string would not be out of place. Most of us have seen the inside of a peg-box with its shapeless tangle of strings, to say nothing of strings on the wrong pegs, or even wound the wrong way round.

We must, of course, bear in mind that we are dealing with 4/4 (or full-size), three-quarter-, half-size, and, in some cases, even smaller violins. It follows, therefore, that the position of the hole in the peg for an E on a half-size violin will be no use at all for a G on a 4/4 size violin, assuming that one uses a normal length string on the small violin. In this case the hole must be drilled well away from the inner side of the peg-box, possibly half way across. The reasons for this are two-fold:

(1) As the string is too long for a small instrument it follows that there will be more turns around the peg.

(2) As the peg is smaller in diameter there will be still more turns round the peg.

As the string should be touching the inside of the peg-box when tuned up to pitch, there is a considerable risk of damage to the peg-box on a small instrument when a normal 4/4 length of string is used. When the string is put on properly the effect is for the string to pull the peg inwards, i.e. to tighten it; therefore, if one were to put, for example, a 4/4 G on to a half-size violin without making allowances for the length of the string, the result could be a crack in the side of the peg-box, necessitating a rather awkward and unnecessary repair.

To avoid the risk of damage to the instrument, and also to prevent having a very untidy-looking peg-box with lots of spare ends of string waving about, there is a simple preventive measure so obvious that perhaps we do not always see it, and that is to shorten the string by cutting a few inches off the peg end!

A good guide for the length of string required for small violins is to measure the distance between the adjuster (assuming that metal strings are fitted), and the peg to which the string is to be attached, and then to add about four inches (102 mm.).

Whilst all the above measurements for drilling the hole are practicable, one must use one's common sense, because all violins are different and each one must be treated as an individual instrument. Plate 5 illustrates what the inside of a peg box ought to look like when the strings are put on in the proper way.

## FITTING PEGS—CELLO

This is done in exactly the same way as on a violin or viola, and is perhaps a little simpler, as it is easier to see what progress one is making since the pegs are much larger. At the same time it is just as important, perhaps even more so, that the fit of the pegs in the holes be exact, in view of the tension of the strings.

As when fitting an odd peg on a violin or viola, try to make it match the others in terms of distance between the outer cheeks of the peg-box and the inner edge of the thumb piece.

When fitting a complete set of pegs the distances between the peg-box and the thumb-piece will be as follows:

| | |
|---|---|
| Full-size | $1\frac{1}{8}''$ (29 mm.) |
| Three-quarter-size | $1\frac{1}{16}''$ (27 mm.) |
| Half-size | $1''$ (25 mm.) |

# CHAPTER 3

## FITTING A BRIDGE—VIOLIN AND VIOLA

Violin and, to a certain extent, viola bridges are obtainable in various grades of quality, ranging from what are known as Dresden—about the cheapest—to the individually hand-cut, expensive types. Somewhere in between lies the type which is best suited to your purpose, and it should, when fitted, support the strings without bending or warping, and be sufficiently hard to prevent metal strings, especially the E on a violin, from cutting their way downwards. If this were to happen, the distance between the surface of the fingerboard and the underside of the string would be reduced, causing the strings to buzz on the fingerboard, especially when stopped notes are played.

These bridges are supplied either fitted or unfitted.

An explanation of these terms is perhaps desirable. An unfitted bridge will have its feet untouched and they will, therefore, look rather thick and chunky. Plate 6 shows the difference quite clearly. It shows an unfitted cello bridge—as usually supplied—and a cello bridge after fitting. The feet on unfitted violin and viola bridges resemble those on the cello bridge. On a fitted bridge some of this wood will have been removed from the feet, but even so a certain amount of fitting of the feet to the belly will be required, as not all instruments are the same shape.

If one is putting on an unfitted bridge, some of the wood on the top curve of the feet may have to be removed or the bridge will look rather clumsy. This surplus wood can be removed with a round 'rat-tail' type of file.

There is another type of bridge available for all the violin family, and that is the De Jacques, with adjustable feet, made by J. Thibouville-Lamy, and sold by most violin shops. These are more expensive than the standard type of bridge, but there is very little, and sometimes nothing, to do by way of fitting. This eliminates the time spent on fitting an ordinary bridge.

A fault frequently found on violin bridges is when someone has put the E and G nicks very near the edges, and simply spaced out the D and A equally. This makes the spaces between the strings too wide, as will be readily appreciated when a small pupil, or one with thin fingers, tries, unsuccessfully, to play a perfect fifth. This fault, on a cello or double bass, makes life even more difficult. It is therefore most important to have all the measurements exact when fitting a bridge. (See table of measurements on p. 55.)

The device illustrated in Plate 7 is intended to simplify the fitting of the feet of a bridge to a violin or viola (See Coda). The cello and double bass bridges, being much larger, require a different technique, described on pp. 23 to 27. The shaping of the top of the bridge is dealt with later.

STEP I

Remove strings and tail-piece so that the top of the violin is exposed. The instrument should be lying on a flat surface which, in turn, should be well covered by a cloth or piece of felt to prevent scratching of the varnish, etc. Better still, partly fill a plastic bag or pillow-case with fine sawdust— easily obtained from a timber yard, joiner, or school wood-work department—and stitch it along its open end. Lay the instrument on this bag and work it about until the instrument remains steady; this stops it rocking to and fro on account of the shape of its back. The instrument must, of course, be level, or the fitting of the bridge will be all wrong.

STEP 2

Slacken off the screw of the bridge-fitting guide. Hold the guide in your right hand and the bridge in your left hand so that the central portion of the tail-piece side of the bridge is closely pressed to the sandpaper side of the bridge-fitting guide. (When a name, e.g., Aubert, is stamped on a bridge, it is customary for this side to face the fingerboard. In the case of an unfitted bridge, either side will do, as they are both at equal angles to the feet.) Now place both bridge and guide, with its felt strip downwards, onto the belly of the instrument and adjust the slide so that the bridge leans very slightly backwards towards the tail-piece; then tighten the screw. (See Plate 8.)

STEP 3

Now place a piece of sandpaper face upwards across the belly of the instrument, holding it tightly with finger and thumb of left hand between the nicks of the $f$ holes. An abrasive sheet obtainable from most ironmongers and manufactured by Cintride of Sheffield in two grades, medium and fine, is really better than sandpaper as it lasts much longer. (See Plate 17.) (If using this Cintride sheet, which is made of metal, it is advisable to glue a piece of material on the back to prevent it from scratching the instrument.)

STEP 4

Holding the bridge on the bridge-fitting guide in the right hand, as described in step 2, with the felt strip resting on the belly, rub the feet of the bridge from side to side across the sandpaper (see Plate 9) until the feet of the bridge conform to the shape of the belly. When the bridge stands up by itself and there are no gaps between the belly and the underside of the feet of the bridge, the first stage in fitting the bridge is completed.

We now turn to the shaping of the top of the bridge. This is just as important as the fitting of the feet, because, if the curve is too flat, the player will sometimes find himself bowing on three strings at once, which is not always desirable! If the curve, on the other hand, is too acute, then the player will have to describe too big an arc with the bow when crossing the strings.

STEP 5

Replace the strings and tailpiece, taking care to put a piece of cloth or paper under the tailpiece (an empty string packet is excellent), especially if the instrument is fitted with adjusters. This prevents any scratching of the varnish, which not only looks unsightly but detracts from the value of a good instrument. The pegs should be turned so that the strings are only just in tension.

STEP 6

Holding the bridge between the first finger and thumb of one hand, place it under the strings with the feet of the bridge in their approximate position. (See Plate 10.) The bridge will be leaning towards the fingerboard. Place the strings in the nicks on the top of the bridge (if there are any; if not, make your own nicks by using a knife-edge file). The spaces between the nicks on the bridge are as follows:

| | |
|---|---|
| Full-size violin | $\frac{7}{16}''$ or 11 mm. |
| Three-quarter-size violin | $\frac{13}{32}''$ or 10·5 mm. |
| Half-size violin | $\frac{13}{32}''$ or 10·5 mm. |
| Viola | $\frac{1}{2}''$ or 12·5 mm. |

Now, gently but firmly, raise the bridge to an upright position. (See Plate 11.)

This usually shows quite clearly that the strings are well above the fingerboard at the bridge end, a state of affairs which is not conducive to good or easy fingering on the part of the teacher, much less the pupil, especially if this happens to be a young child.

STEP 7

The two main measurements to be borne in mind are those relating to the two outer strings and are taken from the face of the fingerboard at the bridge end to the underside of the string. These measurements are as follows for violin and viola  respectively:

Violin: E $\frac{1}{10}''$ or 2·5 mm.    G $\frac{5}{32}''$ or 4 mm.
Viola: A $\frac{1}{8}''$ or 3 mm.       C $\frac{3}{16}''$ or 4·5 mm.

Starting with the E string file downwards through the nick, using a knife-edge file (usually used only for the E), or a round needle-point file. Check the distance between the fingerboard and the underside of the string, and stop filing just before that distance is reached (2·5 mm. for a violin E). Now repeat this process for the G string using this time a round file only, since the nick made by the knife-edge file is too thin for the string to fit into. Again stop just before reaching the required distance, this time 4 mm.

STEP 8

The two middle strings must now be lowered, and this can be done in two ways:

(1) By using a template to mark the shape of the top, the edge of the template touching the nicks for the E and G (see p. 57).

The D and A nicks are then filed down a little at a time, making repeated checks to ensure that one does not go too deep, otherwise the whole process would have to be started again with a new bridge.

(2) It is possible to gauge the correct curve of the top of the bridge without using a template. (Bear in mind the earlier remarks about bowing, particularly the crossing of strings.) The method of doing this is to sight across the strings thus:

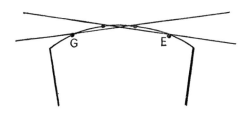

File the D and A nicks down, as in step 8 (2) above, until the space between the underside of the D and an imaginary line over the G and A is approximately the same as the thickness of the D or A string.

STEP 9

The next stage is the removal of the surplus wood from the top of the bridge. This can be done with a knife or chisel, but be sure to work from the centre outwards. Do not try to remove too much wood at a time or there will be a risk of splitting the bridge. When the surplus wood has been removed it is possible that the bridge may be too thick on top at the G and E sides. If so, it will look something like Plate 12.

The front of the bridge (the side facing the fingerboard) can be filed down at the sides so that the top edge is eventually parallel, about $\frac{1}{16}''$ thick. In the illustration below the shaded portions usually need to be removed.

The top of the bridge should then be smoothed with sandpaper and the edges of the ends of the bridge removed with a knife or smooth file. The enlarged diagram below shows what the bridge should look like with its corners removed, when viewed from above.

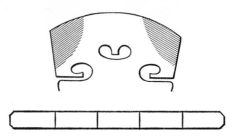

The nicks should be rubbed with a soft pencil, the graphite from which will enable the strings to move easily when being tuned.

Please note that the side of the bridge facing the tailpiece should always remain flat, and on no account must it be bevelled off.

Keep a regular check on the position of the bridge to see that it always is upright. This is best done when tuning the instrument.

It is perhaps convenient to mention at this point the spacing of the strings at the nut end of the fingerboard, between the surface of fingerboard and the underside of the string. The main point to bear in mind is that the strings should be free to vibrate without touching the fingerboard. An approximate guide is to leave a space about the thickness of the string.

One often finds that the strings are too far from the fingerboard at the nut end. This makes it very difficult for a pupil to press the string down without great physical effort, which can easily lead to a bad left hand position.

As the instruments get bigger this problem increases, until on the double bass it is sometimes almost impossible to press the strings down at all.

To remedy this, the needle-point files must be used to

lower the nicks in the nut, taking care to ensure that the groove is flat from front to back, with the back edge rounded off as a precaution against the sharp edge wearing the string, thus:

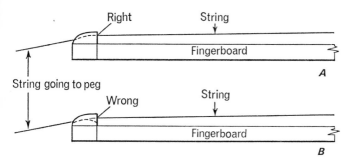

From this it will be readily seen that if the nut is wrongly filed, as in diagram B, the vibrating string length will be fractionally longer than it should be, with consequent problems of faulty intonation.

Having filed the nicks down to their correct depth, remove the surplus wood from the top of the nut, reducing it until the nick is just sufficient to hold the string in position. This wood can be filed off first, using a smooth file, and then finished off with fine sandpaper.

Occasionally, fingerboard nuts, saddles, and fingerboards themselves are made of hardwood stained black to simulate ebony. In this case, filing down the nut will often remove the stained part, which can then be re-stained. A black felt tipped marking pen is ideal for the purpose, and the best type is one with waterproof ink.

## FITTING A BRIDGE—CELLO AND DOUBLE BASS

Unlike violin bridges, which can be bought fitted or unfitted—see previous section—cello bridges are usually supplied with unfitted feet. One can, of course, use a De Jacques bridge, which, though more expensive to buy, has virtually no work to be done on it.

Just as when fitting a bridge to a violin, the cello must be lying on its back, with the scroll to the left, on a piece of cloth on a flat surface, or on the bag described on p. 17. Place the bridge in position, between the $f$ hole nicks, bearing in mind that the only allowable movement backwards, i.e. towards the tail-piece, or forwards, towards the fingerboard, is within the thickness of the bridge in relation to the nicks, thus:

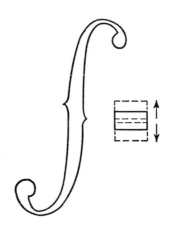

The dotted lines indicate the extent to which the bridge may be moved either backwards or forwards.

The basic position of the bridge is when the centre of the foot on the C side is directly over the highest point of the bass bar, the position of which, unfortunately, varies in different instruments. This is why it is necessary sometimes to move the bridge as shown in the diagram.

Now, holding the bridge in position with one hand, take a short stub of sharply pointed pencil, about 2″–3″

1　*Peg shaper*

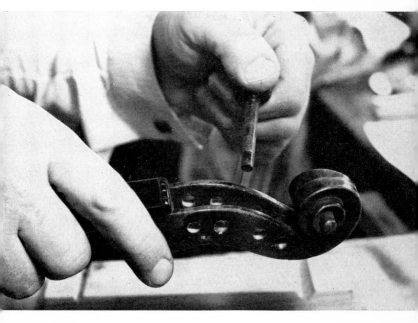

2　*Peg fitted and ready to go into hole*

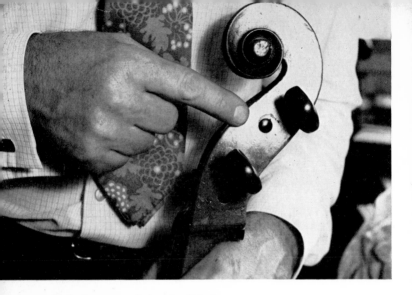

3 *End of peg smoothed and polished*

4 *Hole for string being drilled in peg*

5   *View of peg-box showing correct fitting of strings*

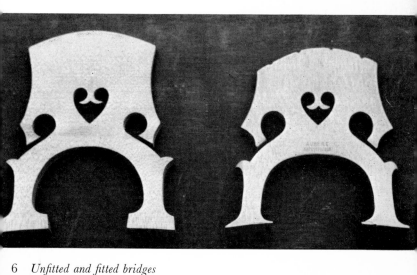

6   *Unfitted and fitted bridges*

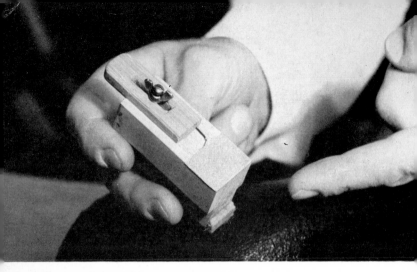

7 *Bridge-fitting guide*

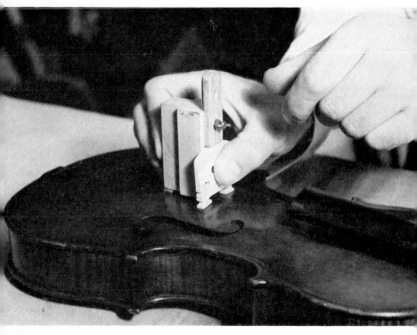

8 *Guide being adjusted for correct angle of bridge*

9  *Bridge ready to have feet rubbed down*

10  *Bridge with feet fitted ready to be pulled up*

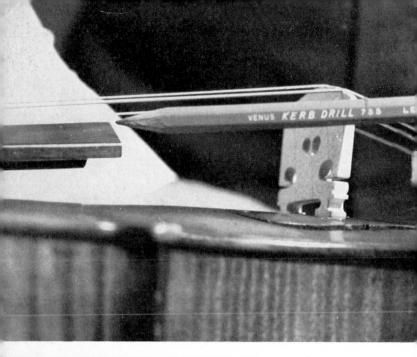

11 *Space too great under string*

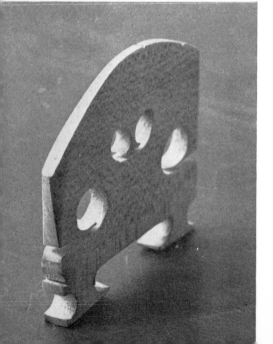

12 *View of top of bridge*

13   *Scribing round feet of cello bridge*

14   *Measuring for length of sound-post*

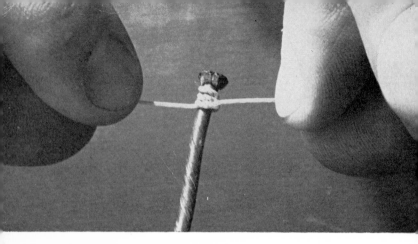

15 *Tying thread round tail-gut*

16 *Position of hands when re-springing bow*

long, in the other hand and scribe round the long sides of the feet of the bridge. These lines can then be joined by using a rule across the ends of the feet. The scribing is done by holding the pencil flat on the belly, and marking round the feet by sliding the pencil round. (See Plate 13.) This reproduces the shape of the belly on the feet of the bridge; hence the need for a short pencil, which will follow the curve of the belly accurately. Do this marking with great care, making sure that the pencil line continues evenly round the feet, as the subsequent fitting of the feet depends on this being right.

Remove the bridge from the instrument, and with a sharp knife pare away the wood from the lower side of the feet. It will generally be easier if the surplus wood is sawn off first, leaving less to be removed with the knife. Great care must be exercised, in the removal of this wood, not to go past the pencil line, or the feet will not fit properly. Make sure that the surface of the feet across the narrow side is exactly flat, thus:

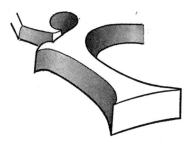

If sufficient care has been taken with the removal of the surplus wood, the feet of the bridge should now fit the belly.

Place the bridge in position, and if there are any gaps between the feet and the belly, pare or scrape off minute particles of wood from the parts of the feet where there are no gaps, until the feet fit all round. The knife used for this operation should have a stiff blade and be very sharp. If necessary, the fitting of the feet can be finished off with a guide, similar to that used for the violin.

The removal of surplus wood from the top of the bridge, and from the side facing the fingerboard is done in the same way as the violin bridge; there is just more of it! The nicks should be $\frac{11}{16}''$ apart, measuring from the centres.

When fitting a double bass bridge one proceeds in the same way as with the cello, except that even more care must be taken to see that the feet really do fit the belly, which may have slight indentations in it, caused by badly fitted previous bridges.

The nicks for the strings on the double bass bridge should be about $1\frac{1}{4}''$ between centres, as basses vary such a lot in size.

Owing to the different shape of the cello and double bass bridges, there is another part which usually needs rounding off; that is, the portion which juts out about half-way up from the feet. It is wise to round off the corners as a precaution against pulling the bridge down if a loose cover catches on them when being taken off.

There is a rather interesting phenomenon, peculiar to the double bass, which I feel is worthy of mention. Many of the double basses at present in use in schools throughout the country are described as being laminated. This is merely another name for plywood which, perhaps, does not sound quite so attractive to the prospective buyer! However, by the nature of the material, the shape of the back and belly have to be pressed out under pressure and heat. It follows, therefore, that if a double bass is stored in a room which is very warm, something is going to happen to the front and back of the instrument, owing to the pressure of the bridge on the belly.

When wood is heated it can be bent, as in bentwood

chairs, and bows, the springing of which is done when the bow is hot. Consequently, in a warm room the plywood of the double bass will soften, and as the sound-post is rigid it will try to push its way through the back of the instrument, which will eventually look as if it has developed a boil, with quite a considerable swelling, looking from the side, like this:

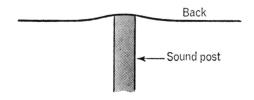

Also, the belly will tend to flatten between the $f$ holes, as the space left when they are cut out reduces the lateral (sideways) strength of the belly.

The net result of this is that the strings will gradually move nearer the fingerboard, necessitating the use of packing pieces of card under the feet of the bridge (see p. 8), or the fitting of a new bridge.

I am at present experimenting with this problem, and during the past couple of years or so have packed up the bridges of two double basses to as much as $\frac{1}{4}''$! I intend to see how much further movement—if any—takes place during the coming months (or years), because so far, a new bridge would have had to be fitted, had it not been for the cardboard packing.

A suggestion I would make to the manufacturers of these double basses is that, instead of the backs and fronts being made of one piece of 5 mm. ply, they should be made of two thinner pieces of ply, glued together at the pressing out stage; they should then be more rigid, and therefore less prone to distortion.

# CHAPTER 4

## FITTING A SOUND-POST

Of all the adjustments necessary from time to time on stringed instruments, the one which probably causes the most frustration and annoyance is the setting up of a sound-post; yet, with the proper equipment, it is really quite simple. The tools needed are as follows:

(a) Fine tooth saw (see Frontispiece)
(b) Smooth file—6″ or 8″
(c) Sound-post setter.

The actual fitting of a new sound-post—as distinct from the setting up of one which, for some reason or other, has fallen down—requires a certain amount of skill, but again it is an operation which every teacher should be able to do, so take heart and read on!

The first thing to do in fitting a new sound-post is to measure the approximate length—a seemingly impossible task, as you need to know the internal distance between the two plates. Have a piece of wood ready, thinner than the sound-post, and insert it in the top loop of the $f$ hole on the E side, until the end touches the back. With a pencil put a mark on this piece of wood level with the belly. (See Plate 14.) Using this as a guide, cut the sound-post to the same size, being careful not to split the edges. File a bevel on each end to correspond with the contours of the front and back of the instrument (bearing in mind that when it is in position, the grain of the sound-post must be at right angles to that of the belly). Insert the sharp edge of the setter into the side of the sound-post, about a third of the way down. It will be readily appreciated that, as the ends of the sound-post are bevelled, it can only fit one way, but to avoid confusion the illustration shows the sound-post with the setter in position, prior to putting it through the *f* hole.

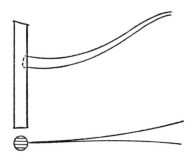

Put the sound-post in through the *f* hole and place it in its position just behind the foot of the bridge on the E side. The diagram below illustrates the correct position of the sound-post.

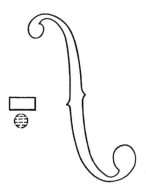

When the sound-post is in its place carefully withdraw the setter. If you find that the sound-post has gone too near the centre of the instrument it means that it is too long, and will therefore need filing a little more until it fits into its proper place.

I must emphasize here that only the correct type of wood, which is straight-grained Swiss Pine, should be used, so that the sound-post will perform its function efficiently. I have seen various objects which some mis-guided people have used for sound-posts—pieces of pencil, dowel, etc.—but these are useless.


## FITTING A NEW TAIL-PIN

There is not a great deal to be said about this operation that has not been dealt with in the section on fitting pegs (p. 10).

The main difference, of course, is that the tail-pin is being fitted into a solid piece of wood, namely the bottom block, instead of into two pieces, as in the peg-box. The taper is the same as that of the pegs, so it is a fairly simple matter to reduce the diameter of the tail-pin until it fits the hole in the block.

Sometimes, of course, it does happen that the hole in the block becomes worn, this being caused by a badly fitted tail-pin. In this case the repairer would use a peg-hole reamer, but in the absence of this tool it is possible to use a round file of about $\frac{3}{8}''$ diameter. If you use a file rotate it anti-clockwise and use it with care, as the hole can very easily be made too large. You will find that it is only the end inch or two of the file that will be used. I must point out that round files will not necessarily have the same taper as a reamer—in fact it is highly unlikely!—hence the need for care.

So long as you bear in mind the fact that the tail-pin should *just* fit, without rocking or wobbling in the hole, then all should be well.

## PUTTING ON A NEW TAIL-GUT

Most string class teachers will, undoubtedly, have had the experience of a pupil arriving at a lesson with the words, 'My violin is broken', only to discover that 'broken' in this case means that the tail-gut has snapped. Hardly anything is more unnerving to a young pupil than the snapping of a tail-gut while he is playing, since the instrument seems to disintegrate before his very eyes. This emphasizes the importance of that 'bit of stuff' round the end-pin which disappears under the tail-piece, and seems to be held in position by magic!

It does not take a great deal of imagination to appreciate that the means of securing the tail-gut to the tail-piece must be very sound, in view of the amount of tension created by tuning the strings, especially metal ones.

For one's own personal use one can do no better than fit one of the nylon types which have two small adjusting screws, allowing the position of the tail-piece to be gauged very accurately. In view of the cost of these, 40p–50p, they are not a practical proposition for use on the normal type of school instrument, and in any case a properly fitted tail-gut is quite efficient and will last for a number of years.

Let us, then, assume that a tail-gut has broken during a lesson, and therefore needs replacing before the pupil takes the instrument home. If it is a class lesson, take this as an opportunity to demonstrate to the pupils what it is that holds everything together, and how.

(1) Remove the tail-piece from the violin, taking care that the adjusters, if fitted, do not scratch the front of the instrument, and take out the old tail-gut. If it sticks, use a pair of pliers to pull it out.

(2) Holding the new piece of tail-gut between finger and thumb, place the end of the gut in a flame (a cigarette

lighter or match is quite suitable), and the heat will cause the gut to swell outwards (see diagram below). When the end begins to bubble slightly, tap this end on to a hard surface, and the end of the tail-gut will now look like this (see diagram), and will be quite hard.

(3) Use strong thread (carpet thread is admirable) and tie it round the gut. Starting from the singed end, and having moistened the thread first to prevent the knots slipping, tie a series of half knots round the gut (about 4 or 5 complete turns, as in Plate 15) and finish with a reef knot as follows. To tie a reef knot hold one end of the thread in each hand, the ends of the thread facing each other thus:

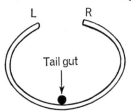

Place the end held in the right hand (R) over the end held in the left hand (L) like this:

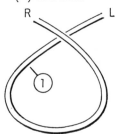

Then pass the end (R) underneath, to come through and over the part marked (1). The knot is then half done and will look like this:

The next step is to place the end marked (R) over the end marked (L).

Finally, pass the end marked (R) underneath the part marked (2) and pull it through. The knot will now appear thus:

The loose ends should now lie in a straight line parallel to the thread. It only remains to pull them tight and the reef knot is complete. Now cut these ends leaving them 6″ long.

(4) Put the opposite end of the tail-gut through one of the holes in the tail-piece, going outwards first, and then push it back through the other hole. To gauge the length required, put the tail-piece in position with the gut round the end-pin, and pull on the loose end of the gut until the bevel at the end of the tail-piece (on the underside) just touches the saddle. This is the piece of ebony at the end of the instrument over which the tail-gut rides when in position. Since it is made of ebony which is very hard, the lower edge of the belly is protected from excessive wear by the tail-gut when the strings are tuned up to pitch.

(5) Holding the tail-gut onto the tail-piece between finger and thumb, remove the tail-piece from the instrument, and cut off the surplus gut, about $\frac{3}{8}$″ from the edge of the hole. This is so as to leave enough gut for singeing and tying the thread round, as in Plate 15. Now put the tail-piece on the instrument to check the finished length of tail-gut, and, if it is too long, simply take up the extra length by tying more knots round the gut. Finally, loop the end of the tail-gut round a solid object (like a water tap), and pull hard on the tail-piece. Great care must be taken to see that the pull on the tail-gut is dead straight, or there will be a considerable risk of breaking the tail-piece by pulling the middle out (between the gut), especially if the tail-piece is made of a softer wood stained black to simulate ebony. Incidentally, if the tail-gut breaks during a lesson, the pupil can hold the new one while you tie the knots. Failing this, hold the gut between your teeth!

When finally in position, the tail-piece should be level with the end of the violin. Exceptions to this are tail-piece tuners, which as a rule have instructions for fitting supplied with them.

# FITTING A TAIL-WIRE ON A DOUBLE BASS

Because of the size of the instrument, it is not practicable to use ordinary tail-gut. We must therefore look elsewhere for some means of holding the tail-piece in position.

One material used is copper wire, of about 10 gauge, i.e. $\frac{1}{10}''$ diameter or 2·5 mm., or slightly thicker. This will hold for quite some time, but can and does break as a result of metal fatigue. This is what happens when tensions or pressures are applied to metal which are beyond the strength of the metal itself, and is a very sound reason why we should not tighten metal strings above the normal pitch at which the string is intended to be played (apart from the slight variations in pitch when tuning). A type of wire which I find very useful is galvanised cable, of about $\frac{1}{8}''$ (3 mm.) diameter. This is very strong, and if correctly fitted will last more or less indefinitely.

Now to the method of fitting this wire on to the tailpiece. Just as with the other stringed instruments, the tail-piece should be level with the end of the instrument. The length of wire needed can be measured by using a piece of ordinary string, preferably of a type which does not stretch. Add on 6″ (153 mm.) to the length from tail-piece to tail-pin and back again.

First of all put the wire through the tail-piece, leaving one long end, and one short end. When these go over the saddle the short end should bend over the ribs about 4″ (102 mm.), or be long enough to reach the end-pin without going round it.

A pair of pliers is necessary for the next stage, which is to unravel about 3″ (76·5 mm.) from each end of the wire, which will now look something like this:

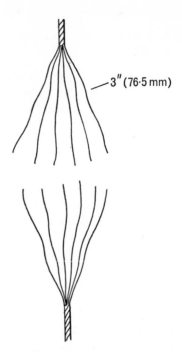

These loose ends must now be plaited together. Fingers can be used at first, but eventually you will have to use pliers, to tighten everything together. To give added strength to the join, two or three of the loose ends of wire can be bent half way and looped round each other, as in the diagram.

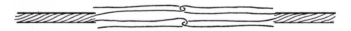

The wire should now appear thus:

The join can then be bound as tightly as possible with something like insulating tape, which covers up all the ends. This will suffice, provided the plaiting is done effectively enough, but to make a really secure join, there are two other possibilities.

The first of these, and the best, as the join will still have flexibility, is to solder it. I do not propose to go into details about soldering, because those who can do it will know anyway, and those who can't will have neither the equipment nor the necessary skill.

The other is to use adhesive which makes use of resin with a hardener. Full instructions are usually enclosed with this type of adhesive, any of which is suitable for the purpose.

Cleanliness is essential, whichever method is used, and for the above mentioned type of adhesive the ends of the wire should be cleaned with detergent, using boiling water, as all traces of grease or dirt must be removed. Be sure to dry the wire thoroughly after washing it, using a clean cloth.

After the adhesive has been worked well into the join, bind it round tightly with insulating tape, and leave to set. This kind of adhesive sets more quickly if heat is applied, e.g. on top of a radiator. It only remains to check that the wire is bent in the correct place to fit over the saddle, and the tail-piece can be replaced on the instrument.

# CHAPTER *5*

## RE-FIXING THE BUTTON ON A BOW SCREW

The need to re-fix the button on the screw is generally the result of the over-tightening of the bow, when the button simply drops off the end of the screw. It can quite often be replaced and tapped gently into position with a light hammer, when it will remain firmly fixed. Do not hit it too hard, for obvious reasons! If it comes off again when the bow is screwed up it is obviously too loose, and a thin sliver of wood put in first will often suffice to hold it in place. Once again care is needed, for the sliver of wood only needs to be the slightest bit too thick and there will be a risk of splitting the button.

It is important to try to keep the screw centrally placed in the button to ensure a correct fit of the button on the end of the stick. Sometimes a tiny spot of glue in the hole also helps, but do not use too much or the increase in pressure when tapping in the screw can split the button.

Perhaps it is interesting to note that the normal fit of the shank of the screw in the button is, quite literally, a square peg in a round hole. The idea is that the corners of the square 'bite' into the round hole thus:

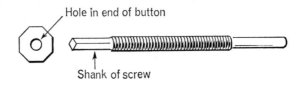

Hole in end of button

Shank of screw

# RE-SPRINGING A BOW

It is with some misgivings that I have included this section, as the springing of a bow is an extremely delicate operation, requiring a true eye, and skill combined with experience, and is fraught with danger. However, as the type of bow with which string-class teachers are dealing is usually of cheap quality, it is therefore prone to losing its spring, especially after being tightened excessively and left like that for long periods.

How all too familiar is the sight of a bow with hair and stick parallel, even before being tightened up for playing! Think of the instruction, 'Turn the screw until the space between the hair and the stick at the narrowest point is wide enough to get a pencil through (see p. 3), and then try to do it on a bow where the space is already about $\frac{3}{4}''$; it is futile! You yourself would not attempt to play with such a bow. Neither should a pupil be expected to. The expression 'Oh!, it's plenty good enough for him, he's only a beginner' is just not to be tolerated, because it is imperative that the beginner has a properly fitted up instrument and bow. He has enough difficulties to cope with without adding to his troubles with a badly fitted up instrument and a poor bow.

Now to the gentle art of springing the bow. The first thing you need is some form of heat. A coal fire is, perhaps, most convenient, but in these days of increasing central heating, open fires are not so readily available. One must therefore look elsewhere; radiant heat gas or electric fires are suitable, but convector heaters are not. Personally, I use the eye-level grill on my wife's gas cooker. This I find ideal, as the heat is instantly available and controllable, and is all round heat, since heat is also reflected upwards from the plate on which a grill pan rests.

The whole length of the bow, apart perhaps for an inch or two at either end, must be heated until it is almost as hot as boiling water.

Extreme care must be taken at this stage not to blister the varnish; spirit varnish will show signs of this sooner than oil varnish. The bows in the Chinese outfits will almost certainly show some signs of blistering, even with very moderate heat, but as the shape of the bow is the important factor, we must accept this philosophically.

We now come to the actual springing of the stick. The frog will have been taken off first, and you must make sure that it is not allowed to slip through the hair, or else the bow will need re-hairing as well.

The actual springing point is about one-third of the way from the head of the bow, so make sure that the stick is hot for some distance at each side of that area. Assuming that you possess a good bow yourself, use that as a guide to copy from. Cello and double bass bows tend to be sprung nearer the middle than violin and viola bows, but if you tackle a bass bow, do make sure that it is hot enough, as, being much thicker than a violin bow, this will take much longer —and the best of luck!

Hold the bow in both hands, across the fingers, which are on the inside, i.e. the side facing the hair, the left hand near the point and the right hand just in from where the frog fits. The thumbs will now be on top of the stick, ready to press downwards simultaneously, so that the stick will bend slightly further than its final position, and hold it like this for a few minutes. (See Plate 16.) The stick must be straight when viewed from the top; in fact this is when one would straighten a bent stick.

Do use extreme care when doing the actual springing, as the grain of the wood on some cheap bows is such that they split, or break, remarkably easily.

Check your progress by slipping the frog on the stick,

to see that the stick is straight—see above—and that the sprung portion of the stick is gradually getting nearer the hair. When it touches the hair, and the stick is straight, leave until cold, and replace the frog—assuming that your bow is still in one piece! It is also a good plan to sight along the stick, facing a window, or light, to give a further check on the straightness of the stick.

Before heating the stick, get the 'feel' of it by gently bending it, and after it is heated, I hope that you will feel the difference in the spring. Although the stick will be extremely hot to handle, do not be tempted to wear gloves.

I do hope that this chapter is of some use, and I suggest practising on some old bows first.

One final reminder: *be careful and do not hurry.*

# CHAPTER 6

## MINOR REPAIRS

Having dealt with the various fittings of the violin—pegs, bridge, tail-gut, and end-pin—we now turn to what might loosely be termed 'glueing up'. Here lurks danger because an instrument can so easily be damaged by the slightest misuse of either cutting tools or cramps. I shall deal with only a minimum of repairs—in fact, only those which it is possible for the teacher to do, with limited resources of both time and equipment.

First of all, a word about glues. Recently I read an advertisement about a new type of adhesive which, according to the claims of the manufacturer, would stick almost anything. This is invaluable when doing carpentry or mending a broken vase, etc., but it is no use on a violin and must never be used in the repair of instruments. Remember that one sometimes has to take a violin apart by removing the belly, and this cannot be done properly if it is glued with epoxy resin, impact adhesives, or anything in fact which is not soluble in water.

There are two makes of tube glue which one can use for emergency repairs, both being soluble in water. These are Croid Clear Liquid Glue and Seccotine. I think the former, being clear, is perhaps more suitable. Whilst not wishing to labour the point, I must stress the utmost importance of using *only* glue which is soluble in water. Normally, in repairing, one uses what is known as animal, or skin, glue.

One of the most common causes of a buzz or rattle is when a portion of the belly or back of the instrument comes unglued. Provided that only a short piece of either of the plates is undone, glueing it back is a fairly straightforward job. Even so, I have had to dig out glue many times from so-called repairs which had been left in a horrible mess.

For simple glueing operations you will need the following:

(1) A tube of glue.
(2) A thin knife, e.g. an old kitchen knife.
(3) Cramps (the number required depends on how much of the front or back is to be glued; four is a useful number).
(4) A receptacle containing hot water.
(5) A dish cloth.

Let us assume that about three inches of the belly is loose, say, on the lower bout on the E side. It will most likely be about half-way between the corner and the bottom blocks, having possibly been caused by a slight knock against a table—heaven forbid—or even by being dropped.

The loose part can usually be found by tapping with the knuckles, when a slight 'clacking' sound will be heard, as distinct from the normal, quite solid sound.

The first thing is to remove any traces of old glue which, of course, will be dry and hard. For this an old knife, such as a table knife, which must be thin, is required. Have the hot water nearby, dip the knife in it frequently, and rub the knife, whilst wet, to and fro in the join between belly and ribs; this will eventually soften the glue and clean the joint.

Cleanliness of any wood which is to be joined by glueing is essential, as otherwise the two surfaces will not come close together. The diagram below will serve to illustrate what a carelessly glued joint looks like.

D*

The jagged lines represent dried glue. It will, therefore, be easily seen that these two surfaces could not possibly fit close together. Do exercise patience when cleaning out old glue, as this is a task which cannot be hurried. Try to avoid letting water run on to other glued parts, because this could melt the glue and, as a result, these parts could open.

The joint has now been cleaned of its glue and must be left to dry. It will then be ready for the glueing up, so again have the hot water nearby and, using the same thin knife, work some of the glue into the join, wiping off any excess with a cloth wrung out in hot water. Apply the cramps round the edge, keeping them close together, and screw up gently until glue squeezes out from the join. Then remove the cramps singly, and wipe away all traces of glue, putting the cramps back as each bit is cleaned. Leave for several hours or, preferably, overnight; then the cramps can safely be removed.

In the event of a much longer section of the belly being unglued, e.g. the whole of the lower bouts from the corner on the G side to the corner on the E side, the basic principle is the same, except that one would glue the belly on to the bottom block first, taking care to see that, before cramping, the fit of the ribs round the belly is equal all the way round. Here it must be emphasized most strongly that *all* traces of old glue must be removed, especially from the block. This will take much longer than removing glue from the ribs of the large surface of the block as compared with the edge of the ribs.

I once had a double bass to attend to which had a most annoying buzz, and evidence of this could be heard by tapping with one's knuckles at various points on the belly. Finally, after a very close examination and much deliberation, it was decided that the belly would have to come off. Only then was it discovered that the cause of the buzz was dried glue between the top block and the belly (under the fingerboard) which had not been thoroughly cleaned off during a previous removal of the front, and which was therefore allowing the belly to vibrate. Proper cleaning off of old glue, and careful cramping, would have averted the removal of the belly in this case.

Incidentally, it is a good plan to put cramps on dry before glueing up, just to make sure that everything fits as it should.

Another fairly common place in which to find cracks is in what are termed the wings of the $f$ holes. These cracks are easily caused by some form of downward pressure, such as a shoulder rest carelessly put in the case (near the bridge), or a thick piece of music rolled up and then literally forced into the case.

However, these cracks, provided they are not too extensive, can often be closed up by the use of a piece of cork *carefully* wedged in the $f$ hole. Clear liquid glue is quite suitable for this. Squeeze a small quantity of glue over the crack. Then, by gently pressing down and up on the side of the crack which moves (both sides if necessary), the glue can be gradually worked into the crack.

When inserting the piece of cork, you will see glue squeezing out of the crack, which is a good sign, as this is an indication that glue has gone right into the crack. As previously mentioned, wipe off excess glue with a piece of rag that has been wrung out in hot water. Remember to insert the cork wedge gently.

Occasionally, a fingerboard will come off, as often as not because it has not been properly glued on. This does not mean that one must apply thick strong glue, liberally! Quite the reverse, in fact, for the glue should be fairly thin for this purpose, to facilitate the easy removal of the fingerboard, which is sometimes necessary.

While it is possible to glue on a fingerboard by using one cramp across the middle, bear in mind the fact that the underside of the fingerboard is sometimes slightly convex and therefore only the centre portion of the glueing surface of the fingerboard is really in firm contact with, and thereby glued to, the neck.

I prefer to use three cramps (more on a cello), because I am convinced that this is the only effective way of securing the fingerboard firmly. The illustration below shows the type of cramp which you will need. It is, in fact, a guitar capodastro, which happens to suit the purpose admirably. When used on a small violin, you may have to use a packing piece of cork or similar material on the straight portion.

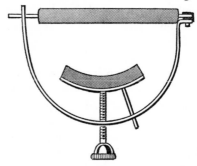

The first step is to remove all traces of old glue. An important point to bear in mind here is that, should a portion of fingerboard remain glued to the neck, it should not be removed as it will serve as a guide when replacing the fingerboard.

Secondly, place the fingerboard in position, dry with all the cramps on, not forgetting pieces of soft wood or cork about $\frac{1}{4}''$ thick as protection for the neck and face of the fingerboard.

While in its liquid form, glue is a remarkably efficient lubricant, as you will discover when cramping the finger-board on! Therefore, exercise great care when replacing the fingerboard to position it *exactly* flush with the sides of the neck, and also centrally on the instrument. The clear glue previously mentioned is probably as good as anything for a fingerboard (apart, of course, from skin glue), as it is fairly thin in consistency, but even this can be thinned a little with water.

In the event of the fingerboard nut coming off by itself (not a very common occurrence), clean off any old glue as usual, and put only a spot of glue on the underside of the nut (the side which is to be glued to the neck). The strings will hold the nut quite firmly in position, so that the tiny spot of glue applied is just sufficient to prevent the nut from slipping sideways.

## MINOR REPAIRS TO VIOLIN OR VIOLA CASES

Some teachers may wish to know something about repairs to cases, and how to replace the handle and fasteners. One always hopes that the pupils' fathers will do these things, but, regrettably, they seldom do.

First, then, a list of the tools you will probably need. Please read on; the list is not a formidable one!

Light hammer (cross pein type)
Bradawl—$\frac{1}{8}''$ diameter
Small screwdriver (about 6''–8'')
$\frac{1}{8}''$ twist drill (if you have a wheelbrace)
Pair of pliers (electrician's type) with jaws that open wide
Quantity of bifurcated rivets, $\frac{1}{8}'' \times \frac{1}{2}''$ and $\frac{1}{8}'' \times \frac{5}{8}''$.

A bifurcated rivet looks like this:

The case fasteners are often troublesome, especially the two end ones, usually of the snap-fastening type. These are normally fixed to the case by small nails, bent over on the inside before the lining is put in. It follows, therefore, that the holes, usually three on the fastener and two on the clip, will be rather small. They will need enlarging to $\frac{1}{8}''$ to accommodate the rivets, which will be inserted to take the place of the original nails. This can sometimes be done with the bradawl, but one often has to use a drill, as the metal is too thick to push a bradawl through.

Having enlarged the holes to the correct size (try a rivet in the hole and see if it fits), place the fastener on the case and with the bradawl make corresponding holes in the case, making sure that the clip is still on the lid! Push one rivet through, and, using the blade of the screwdriver, open the ends of the rivet until the edge of the hammer head will fit into the gap. The flat head of the rivet must then be held against a hard surface, such as an old flat-iron, so that the two ends of the rivet can be hammered flat against the inside of the case.

Putting these rivets in is sometimes a little awkward, but one feels a certain sense of satisfaction when the job is done.

The rivets when finished should look something like this:

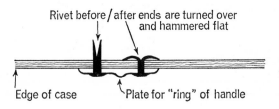

Rivet before / after ends are turned over and hammered flat

Edge of case            Plate for "ring" of handle

Occasionally the handle on cheap cases—often a strip of leather held at either end by metal rings—breaks at one end or the other, usually by the metal ring simply wearing through the leather. If the leather is long enough, it can still be used, by turning the worn end round the ring, and fastening with a bifurcated rivet. For this purpose, a leather punch is useful. Should you not possess one, I feel sure that your colleagues in the Art and Craft department will rise to the occasion.

The same procedure as explained previously is used for putting the rivet through the leather, and it is best to put the head of the rivet on the outside.

Sometimes the metal rings to which the handles are fastened will come out of the clip on the case. This is where the pliers are useful in gripping the ring between the jaws, and gently squeezing the two ends together. If too much force is used, you will distort the ring, and re-shaping it is rather difficult, though by using the pliers, hammer, and a certain amount of ingenuity, it can be done!

All the above remarks refer to the cheaper type of shaped case, usually paper covered and made of fibre-board or similar material. On the old-fashioned wooden 'coffin' type of case, fasteners can generally be screwed on, using very small countersunk wood screws, of sizes about $\frac{3}{8}'' \times$ No. 2 or 3.

One sometimes finds that the piece of card on the inside of the lid of a normal shaped case comes off, generally, I suppose, because when pupils take out the bow, they tend to pull it forward too soon, instead of sliding it out sideways. The card is glued to a small piece of wood, about $\frac{1}{2}''$ square and $1\frac{1}{2}''$ long, which in turn is glued to the lid, and generally fastened with a small pin from outside.

The remedy for this is quite simple. Clean off the old glue from all the surfaces and replace both card and piece of wood, using a rubber-based glue (such as 'P.V.A.'), which sets more quickly than animal glue, and, what is probably more important, is readily available in plastic containers, usually with a nozzle attached, which makes it possible to apply the glue in small quantities, and is easily controllable. This white glue is also most valuable in sticking back the lining of a case which has come loose, whether felt or paper.

There is very little else one can do with cheap cases. I have tried glueing the top of the lid, and the bottom of the case, on to their respective sides, but not with a great deal of success. One really has to decide whether it would not be better (and indeed cheaper, bearing in mind the time one can spend repairing a case) just to replace a badly damaged case with a new one.

## EMERGENCY REPAIRS

(1) *Fingerboard coming off*, e.g. a few minutes before a concert is due to begin. This can be held in position with Sellotape (or similar type of self-adhesive tape), wound right round the fingerboard and neck. Make sure that there are no sticky edges left!

(2) *Sudden bridge collapse* so that it splits across the middle. This can also be taped together with Sellotape on the front and back of the bridge, and it should certainly survive a lesson, or even a concert. Bearing in mind the fact that when the bridge is correctly positioned, all the pressure of the strings is downwards, there is no reason why this emergency measure should not survive 2 or 3 hours of playing, which is roughly the duration of a concert.

(3) *Section of belly or back unglued from ribs.* On a violin or viola, a piece of Sellotape from front to back across the ribs will help to stop the rather annoying buzz that some-times occurs.

On a cello or double bass it is sufficient to take the tape from the belly or back, as the case may be, on to the ribs, making sure that the offending portion is held down while placing the tape in position.

(4) *Metal string breaking at ball end.* Tie a knot on but

before pulling it tight loop it round the adjuster. Turn up the loose end at right angles to the string. This will help to prevent the end from slipping through. (See p. 9.)

If a string breaks in the peg-box, it is sometimes possible to tie a reef knot, provided the knot does not go beyond the fingerboard nut onto the fingerboard. Strings which break in the peg-box of a full sized instrument can be kept and used on smaller instruments.

(5) *An unexplained buzz*

(*a*) If metal strings are fitted, check that the knurled nut which fastens the adjuster on to the tail-piece is screwed firmly down—what is known as finger tight.

(*b*) See that the tuning screw is slightly screwed down; it is a good plan to unscrew adjusters occasionally, and tune up the strings with the pegs. Adjusters which are screwed right down are not only useless in that position, but also constitute a hazard to the instrument, first because they frequently scratch varnish off and sometimes actually wear a hollow in the belly, and second because there is a distinct risk of damage to the instrument in the event of any excess pressure on the tail-piece.

(*c*) If a piece of wire is used instead of tail-gut, as on certain tail-piece tuners, make sure that no loose ends are catching on anything.

(*d*) Check the peg-box for loose ends of string.

(*e*) See that there is sufficient space between chin-rest and tail-piece, and also between chin-rest and belly if the violin is a high model.

(*f*) Tap round the edges of the belly and back to see if they are loose anywhere, and if so, see 3 above.

(6) *Screw of bow slipping through eye in frog.*

(*a*) Take the screw out and remove the frog from the stick. Using the end of the screw (which usually has no thread on it) inserted in the eye, turn the eye half a turn anti-clockwise, taking care to avoid letting the screw touch the thin edge of the metal lining of the frog, which is easily damaged.

(*b*) If a pair of pliers is available, the eye can sometimes be gently squeezed together, which makes it, in effect, slightly elliptical; but do this with care, or the eye will be flattened altogether, and the owner of the bow will be in a worse mess than before!

Whichever of the two methods is used, remember that it is temporary, and a new eye, and probably screw as well, should be put in as soon as possible. Sometimes, but not often, one may find an eye that will fit in the same hole as the old one, but if the hole in the frog is too big for the new eye it will have to be plugged, i.e. filled in, and a new hole drilled.

Great care must be exercised when plugging the hole to prevent the frog from splitting, and when drilling the new hole, to make sure that it is in the centre of the lining of the frog, thus:

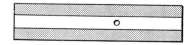

This is to ensure that the frog fits exactly on the stick, and can therefore move easily when the hair is being adjusted for playing.

The reason for the above problem is that screws and eyes come in such a multiplicity of sizes that one can very seldom find a replacement eye to fit the existing screw. May I, therefore, put in a plea to the makers of screws and eyes to standardize the sizes, i.e. the diameter of the threaded portion, and the number of threads per inch or centimetre.

(7) *Adjuster breaking.* Remove from the tail-piece, and put the ball end of the string through the hole in the tail-piece so that the string goes through the slot. If the ball is

too big to go through the hole, then the string will have to be put on afresh, putting it through the tail-piece from underneath.

# CODA

It would appear that some string-class teachers experience difficulties when trying to buy the rather less common 'spare parts' at the local music shop, assuming that there is one. These would include such things as half-size cello pegs, small violin pegs, bow screws and eyes, and so on. These could be supplied by me at 23 Hull Road, Cottingham, Yorkshire, HU16 4PN, generally by return of post. It would be a help, perhaps, if the damaged part, particularly in the case of screws and eyes, could be sent with an order. For cello end-pins the diameter is usually sufficient, as all end-pins are not, unfortunately, the same diameter. In the event of getting one that is too big for the hole, it is sometimes possible to drill out the hole until it fits the pin.

I give here two sets of figures which may be found interesting. Thanks are due for them to a colleague of mine, Mr. Peter Schorah, Head of the Physics Department at Newland High School, Hull, and to the pupils who worked them out.

The tension of the strings pulling on the tail-piece of a violin and double bass respectively are approximately 76 lb. and 77 lb. or 34·8 and 35·046 kg., and the pressure of the bridges on the belly of a violin and double bass are approximately 110 and 76 lb. per square inch, or 7·75 and 5·35 kg. per square cm. These figures, I think, give some idea of the enormous stresses to which stringed instruments are subject, another very sound reason why we, and our pupils, should always take care of our instruments.

# TABLES OF USEFUL MEASUREMENTS

The tables of measurements which follow are based on metal strings of the type known as rope core; metal strings with a solid wire core should be slightly nearer to the fingerboard. In putting the nicks in the nut and bridge, measure straight across, and not round the top of the bridge. Then space out the middle two strings equally.

In giving metric equivalents, I have gone to the nearest $\frac{1}{2}$ mm.; there may be slight variations, depending on the size and shape of the instrument.

## DISTANCE FROM OUTER CHEEK OF PEG BOX TO INNER EDGE OF THUMB-PIECE ON PEG

|  | $\frac{1}{8}$ | $\frac{1}{4}$ | $\frac{1}{2}$ | $\frac{3}{4}$ | 4/4 |
|---|---|---|---|---|---|
| *Violin* | $\frac{3}{8}''$ | $\frac{7}{16}''$ | $\frac{1}{2}''$ | $\frac{9}{16}''$ | $\frac{7}{10}''$ |
|  | 10 mm. | 11 mm. | 13 mm. | 15 mm. | 18 mm. |
| *Viola* |  |  |  |  | $\frac{13}{16}''$ |
|  |  |  |  |  | 20·5 mm. |
| *Cello* |  |  | $1''$ | $1''$ | $1\frac{1}{8}''$ |
|  |  |  | 25 mm. | 27 mm. | 28·5 mm. |

## STRING SPACINGS AT NUT TO CENTRE OF NICKS

| *Violin* | $\frac{1}{2}''$ | $\frac{17}{32}''$ | $\frac{9}{16}''$ | $\frac{19}{32}''$ | $\frac{21}{32}''$ |
|---|---|---|---|---|---|
| (G to E) | 13 mm. | 13·5 mm. | 14 mm. | 15 mm. | 16·5 mm. |
| *Viola* |  |  |  |  | $\frac{13}{16}''$ |
| (C to A) |  |  |  |  | 20·5 mm. |
| *Cello* |  |  | $\frac{21}{32}''$ | $\frac{3}{4}''$ | $\frac{13}{16}''$ |
| (C to A) |  |  | 16·5 mm. | 19·5 mm. | 21 mm. |
| *Double bass* |  |  |  |  | $1\frac{1}{4}''$ |
| (E to G) |  |  |  |  | 32 mm. |

## STRING SPACINGS ON BRIDGE TO CENTRE OF NICKS

| | $\frac{1}{8}$ | $\frac{1}{4}$ | $\frac{1}{2}$ | $\frac{3}{4}$ | 4/4 |
|---|---|---|---|---|---|
| *Violin* | $1''$ | $1\frac{1}{8}''$ | $1\frac{7}{32}''$ | $1\frac{1}{4}''$ | $1\frac{11}{32}''$ |
| (G to E) | 25·5 mm. | 28·5 mm. | 31 mm. | 32 mm. | 34 mm. |
| *Viola* | | | | | $1\frac{1}{2}''$ |
| (C to A) | | | | | 38 mm. |
| *Cello* | | | $1\frac{5}{8}''$ | $1\frac{3}{4}''$ | $2''$ |
| (C to A) | | | 41 mm. | 44·5 mm. | 50·5 mm. |
| *Double Bass* | | | | | $3\frac{1}{2}''$ |
| (E to G) | | | | | 89 mm. |

# DISTANCE BETWEEN SURFACE OF FINGERBOARD (BRIDGE END) AND UNDERSIDE OF STRING

| | 1/8 | 1/4 | 1/2 | 3/4 | 4/4 |
|---|---|---|---|---|---|
| **Violin** — G | 3/32" 2·5 mm. | 1/8" 3 mm. | 5/32" 5 mm. | 3/16" 5 mm. | 3/16" 5 mm. |
| **Violin** — E | 1/16" 2 mm. | 3/32" 2·5 mm. | 1/8" 3 mm. | 1/8" 3 mm. | 1/8" 3 mm. |
| **Viola** — C | | 7/32" 6 mm. | 11/64" 4·5 mm. | 3/16" 5 mm. | 3/16" 5 mm. |
| **Viola** — A | | 5/32" 4 mm. | 1/8" 3 mm. | 1/8" 3 mm. | 1/8" 3 mm. |
| **Cello** — C | 7/32" 6 mm. | 1/4" 6·5 mm. | | | |
| **Cello** — A | 5/32" 4 mm. | 11/64" 4·5 mm. | | | |
| **Double Bass** — E | | | 9/32" 7 mm. | 9/16" 14 mm. | |
| **Double Bass** — G | | | | 11/64" 4·5 mm. | 1/2" 13 mm. |

## SOUND-POST THICKNESSES

| | 1/8 | 1/4 | 1/2 | 3/4 | 4/4 |
|---|---|---|---|---|---|
| **Violin** | 1/8" 3 mm. | 5/32" 3·5 mm. | 5/32" 4 mm. | 7/32" 5 mm. | 1/4" 6 mm. |

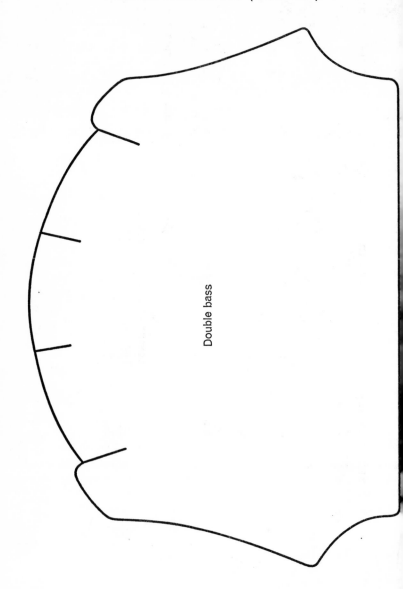

Double bass

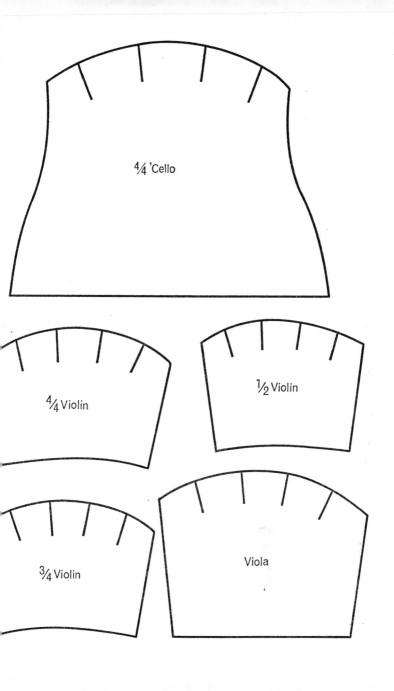

4/4 'Cello

4/4 Violin

1/2 Violin

3/4 Violin

Viola